The 0-6-2 Tank Papers
5600- 5699, 6600-6699
1. 5600-5699

IAN SIXSMITH
Tables by Richard Derry

The Taff Vale had an 'A' class of some sixty 0-6-2Ts, built over the years 1914-21. 305 (numbered 403 till 1947) at Cardiff Queen Street on 16 May 1952, had been rebuilt with a GW No.10 boiler and has even acquired a pannier tank-style toolbox for the front end. R.C. Riley, transporttreasury

Irwell Press Ltd.

Acknowledgements

Gavin Glenister, Brian Penney, Allan C. Baker, Nick Deacon, Peter Coster, Brian Bailey and especially Eric Youldon. Richard Derry once again painstakingly compiled the Allocation Tables.

First published in the United Kingdom in 2017,
by Irwell Press Limited, 59A, High Street, Clophill,
Bedfordshire MK45 4BE
Tel: 01525 861888
www.irwellpress.com

The 0-6-2 Tank Papers
5600-5699, 6600-6699
I. 5600-5699

The Great Western never had to 'combine' with former rivals and equals, like the other companies involved in the Grouping of 1923 did. It didn't amalgamate; it 'absorbed'; there is a difference, and it never had to indulge in struggles for supremacy in locomotive design or practice – the 'Drawing Office Wars' experienced elsewhere. It had merely to impose its way of doing things without much of a second thought and yet Collett proved sensitive to local sensibilities in South Wales – to the remarkable extent that he built a new class of 200 engines! The only appreciably large area of operations the GWR was required to digest after 1923 was the collection of Welsh Valley lines devoted to the transport and export

of its coal. Famously the little town of Barry boasted the biggest coal exporting port in the world by 1913, with Cardiff second. Thereafter, admittedly, it was a story of steady decline; the best part of half of more than 600 pits in South Wales had closed after twenty years and exports by 1947, while substantial enough, were but a fraction of the traffic in its heyday.

The work was simple, in a way; loaded wagons came down the valleys and empties went back up. For much of this coal, along with other freight and passenger work, in fact everything on offer, the companies had, remarkably, arrived at similar versions of a basic 0-6-2 side tank. Of the Barry Railway's 150 or so locomotives, for instance, nearly half

were 0-6-2Ts, including four built in 1899 in the USA. The Cardiff Railway had only 36 locos but a third were 0-6-2Ts while the Rhymney Railway employed some fifty-odd 0-6-2Ts among its 120 or so locos. The Taff Vale Railway, oldest and largest, had 274 locos and the great part of them were 0-6-2Ts.

The story of the GWR's 'culture clash' with the Valley companies is best told, by far, by John C. Gibson in *Great Western Locomotive Design A Critical Appreciation* (David & Charles, 1984). To the Welsh Valley companies the Great Western was a malign force; its own branches infiltrated the Valleys, it monopolised the longer distance onward transport of the coal, to London and the Midlands and exercised undue influence on prices,

It was the Welsh valley companies that established the 0-6-2T as a maid of all work and without them there would not have been the two hundred Great Western versions. The indigenous 0-6-2Ts were not replaced wholesale, not by any means but instead were 'Great Westernised' with fittings and, most significantly, taper boilers, so that many came to resemble 5600/6600 locos; at a glance, at any distance, you'd hardly notice the difference. Old Rhymney Railway 'R' class 0-6-2T, of a class which formed the foundation of Collett's engines, GW number 35, kept its parallel boiler, as we can see here. It is on an engineering train at Cardiff Queen Street on 16 May 1952, with serif BRITISH RAILWAYS. GWR features it has picked up include a 'wind shield' or weatherboard recessed for a lamp, GW style lamp irons and a sliding shutter on the cab. It was withdrawn at the end of 1956. R.C. Riley, transporttreasury

155 (Ex-Cardiff Railway 35) waits in the loop at Cherry Orchard southbound with a goods on 17 May 1952. Great Western-like and yet not... R.C. Riley, transporttreasury

Hard to tell at a distance. Much-transformed Rhymney Railway number 37, GW 80, powers a lengthy up train at Ystrad Mynach on 10 July 1952. There were four engines in this 'AP' class, used on passenger work from Rhymney shed for very many years. No.80 was not withdrawn until 1954. R.C. Riley, transporttreasury

conditions and so on. Once Grouping seemed a reality the Welsh companies gave up on investment and ran their locos and stock into the ground – a scorched earth policy! The exception, notes Gibson, was the Rhymney, which had also built a fine new modern works at Caerphilly. With GWR ownership looming, it probably wished it hadn't. So when Grouping came locomotive matters were in dire straits and Collett was forced to shore things up as best he could. Existing 'crocks' were kept going and engines that would in normal circumstances have been scrapped were reboilered instead, at great expense. The effect was extraordinary, delaying the construction of Castles at Swindon and forcing the GW to put 4300 2-6-0s out to private contractors.

A locomotive for South Wales had already been arrived at, in the form of the 2-8-0Ts (see *The 2-8-0 Tank Papers: 1 4200, 5200 2-8-0Ts, 4200-5294*) but these were not at all popular on the newly annexed Welsh lines; they were new, they were Great Western (in all, more than sufficient to damn them) but practical objections concerned their unsuitable dimensions – too long for turnouts, too wide for platforms. Collett, as Gibson writes, 'had to act quickly'.

He saw no case for a radically different engine type and though pannier tanks, eight-coupled tanks and other types were drafted in, he worked up his own version of the Welsh 0-6-2T maid of all work. The outcome was that the GWR built 200 new 0-6-2Ts (though they didn't all go to South Wales, it is true) while there were still the best part of 200 of the native engines surviving long enough to pass into BR ownership. Some of the reboilered ones at first glance were barely distinguishable from the Swindon model.

No time was wasted; the first drawings were made in August 1924 and the first loco, 5600 appeared in December. Overtime soared in the meantime, in the Drawing Office and on the shop floor. Collett's design recalled the Rhymney 'R' class of 1907 vintage, married of course to a taper boiler, the Standard No.2. The bunker, tanks and cabs were derived directly from the 2-8-0Ts; the only new major component was the cylinder casting. What follows is in the nature of 'now it can be told…'

Just before Christmas 1924 5600 was steamed for the first time; it inched forward only to be brought to a sudden stand by the alarmed driver. 'Groans and shrieks' had emanated from the engine's vitals and the

exhaust had gone haywire. Without quoting Gibson at considerable length, suffice to say that the end of the valve spindle was unsupported and when moved, bent under upthrust, hence the groans.

Catastrophe loomed, for Collett's career not the least; *another forty-nine* 5600s were on order and a dozen in course of erection! The D.O. staff were ordered, literally, back to their drawing boards, there to stay until matters were fixed; at the same time, it was made clear that instant dismissal awaited any wretch who 'blabbed'.

A crude and massive cross member bridging the frames was arrived at, rendering the gear very inaccessible and as a precaution the drawings were dated *August* 1924! It really did never happen. Gibson found out all about it (it was an open secret of course) a few months later, though he was 'sworn to secrecy'. Forty years on with all the players long deceased, he rightly thought there was no harm in the truth at last.

Subsequent evolution of the 0-6-2Ts matched that of the other GW tank classes, though the bunkers were not found to be too small, and did not have to be extended, as was common on earlier classes. Despite the 'emergency' over 5600, all two

A somewhat poignant portrait of Barry Railway 231, an 0-6-2T of that company's 'B' class, dainty engines dating back to 1890. It is at Swindon on 16 December 1950 but had been withdrawn the previous year; there is a somewhat fed-up crewman on board and perhaps like many such doomed tanks, it was serving as a works shunter for a few months before its final demise. The GW-style recessed 'wind shield' has taken a bit of a battering! ColourRail

hundred were built at a crisp rate, aided by contracting 6650-6699 to Armstrong Whitworth, in the four years up to October 1928 (one a week more or less). In a year or two the sliding shutters became standard issue as on all other classes. The bunkers were flat at the back at first but the lamp iron recesses were fitted (again like all other classes) and the 'wind shield' as the crews called it ('weatherboard' to others) also began to appear, though in the end these might not have been universal fitments.

The 6600s were fifteen hundredweights heavier than the 5600s, though the reason seems to have gone unrecorded. It is only possible to surmise that the extra weight was due to modified, heavier, balancing.

Power/Route Classification
Power class D, red disc route availability. BR 5MT – the only tank class so classified? The vagaries of tractive effort and wheel diameter made them the theoretical equivalent of Granges, Halls, Black Fives and the rest and, insofar as it makes sense to talk of tractive effort, ahead of the (twenty ton heavier) BR Class 4 2-6-4Ts. The BR power classifications, it is worth mentioning, were never displayed on WR steam locos.

ATC
Automatic Train Control was fitted to 0-6-2Ts from the 1930s; all the 6600 series had it but far fewer of the earlier 5600s, for some reason.

Livery
Livery at first was green, which was applied down through the years till 1948, apart from the wartime black used 1942-45. The tanksides had GREAT WESTERN in serif, then the GWR shirt button/roundel of 1934 began to appear. From 1942 to 1947 came GWR in block and then afterwards BRITISH RAILWAYS, sometimes serif, sometimes Gill sans. Subsequently they carried the first and second emblems. Green continued to be applied after the War, into 1948, but then they were painted in plain BR black until 1957. From then those more associated with passenger work got plain green. In that year 5696 and 6685, followed by many others, got full lined out dark green. Caerphilly turned out at least

126 of the class in this style until February 1961 from when lining was dropped. Examples of plain green noted from photographs were 5624, 6604, 6622, 6639, 6642. Later the tale had gone full circle when, for example, 5691 was ex-Swindon in 1964 in plain black.

In early 1948 the temporary 'W' suffix was appended to 5641, 5655 and 5688.

> The 0-6-2Ts were built continuously in a single bloc 1924-1928 (with Armstrong Whitworth responsible for a quarter of them) and these Introductory Notes relate to both the 5600 and 6600 series. The historical notes and the various detail differences, liveries and so on, apply equally to all 200 0-6-2Ts. The 6600s have been detailed in a separate volume largely for reasons of space.

Cherry Orchard, south east of Caerphilly, on 17 May 1952 and 38 (ex-Rhymney Railway 42) passes 155 (seen earlier in the loop). R.C. Riley, transporttreasury

5646 at Danygraig in 1935; tall safety valve bonnet and an impressive layer of all-over grey to entirely obscure the plain GW dark green that lies beneath. Somewhere, there are the serif letters that form GREAT WESTERN; the GWR 'shirt button' introduced from 1934 will not come till the next Heavy General which could be several years away. No ATC as yet, though screw coupling stowed out to the way on its hook. Steam heat hose removed leaving open connection next to drawhook. D.K. Jones Collection.

6671 made a brief appearance in the London Division in its first year or two, working from Slough shed. It stands there on 17 May 1930, in green with GREAT WESTERN on the tanks. ATC fitted from new, with the copper cap chimney applied to the class. From 6650 the engines had come out with the shorter safety valve bonnet, as here, though as time went by they could be found intermingled on just about any of the locos. At the front of the tanks a steel hoop curves over the boiler top; this is the 'harness' supporting the tanks either side. 6650 has yet to acquire the sliding shutter for the cab window. H.C. Casserley, courtesy R.M. Casserley.

5609 at Gloucester in 1939, in green with the 'shirt button' emblem which had been introduced in 1934. In this early period the red route disc with D power classification was applied to the sliding shutter rather than on the bunker, above the number plate. D.K. Jones Collection.

6647 at Barry in 1929; green livery, serif GREAT WESTERN, no shutter yet. ColourRail

The post-war 'block' lettering GWR 1: on 5671 at Barry shed on 6 July 1947, before the old Barry Railway building was re-roofed by BR. This is steam loco maintenance in the raw, as widely practised; the front of the loco is resting on a baulk or beam under the front on the frames, which itself is resting on the baulks we see parallel to the engine – there will be another set of timbers on the other side. The loco would have been lifted with the breakdown crane and the front wheelset run out for attention. A couple of axleboxes sit on the ground with various parts left on the running plate; 5671 must have suffered a hot box and is waiting the journals to be machined. A small patch weld has appeared at the front of the tank at the bottom. H.C. Casserley, courtesy R.M. Casserley.

The post-war 'block' lettering GWR 2: on 6660 at Cardiff General with a local, at Riverside down platform 9. As far as can be traced, the target board on 6660 indicates a Cathays (88A at the time) turn working through to Penarth and/or Cadoxton. 6660 lasted at Cathays from 1945 until its withdrawal nearly twenty years later. The station had opened in 1893 as a consequence of the Riverside branch being upgraded for passenger services. It was used by the Taff Vale Railway for its services to Penarth and Cadoxton and by the Barry Railway for its Barry Island, Vale of Glamorgan and Pontypridd services. The station was assimilated into Cardiff General as an island platform (Nos.8 and 9) in the extensive remodelling work of the 1930s. Taper buffer stocks, as fitted to all the classes early on. The bunkers, again like most of the tank classes, started off straight at the back without the recess for the lamp or, later, the 'wind shield' (as crews termed the weatherboard). The process of conversion got underway early in 1935; *The Railway Observer* for instance reporting in that year that: *...the following 56XX AND 66XX Class 0-6-2Ts now have bunkers with tops recessed for the lamp bracket, similar to those fitted to 2-8-0T Nos. 5275-94 when first built: 6652 (noted 24/2/35) and 5606, 6617 (7/4/35).* H.C. Casserley, courtesy R.M. Casserley.

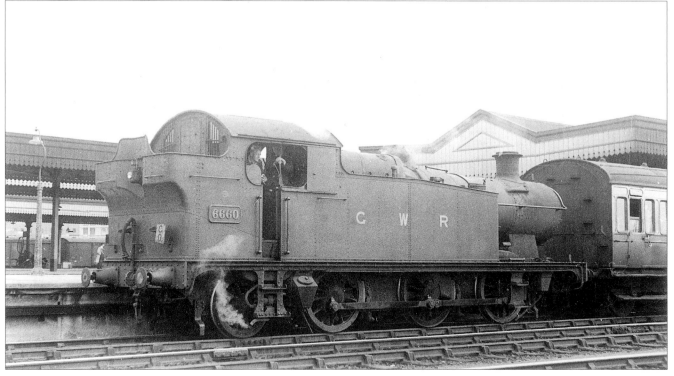

The post-war 'block' lettering GWR 3: on 6629 at Banbury on 20 July 1946. By the smokebox saddle on the right-hand side, ahead of the splasher, a lockable toolbox (useful for the preparation crews) has appeared. Some 40-50 of the 0-6-2Ts acquired one, seemingly from the period of the Second World War or shortly afterwards. Those that were fitted kept them to the end; there were two toolboxes originally in the cabs. H.C. Casserley, courtesy R.M. Casserley.

The post-war 'block' lettering GWR 4: on 5667 at Barry on 6 July 1947. By the splasher (it can be seen both sides, in many illustrations) is one of the front lubricator boxes for the steamchest, slidebars and so on. On most GWR engines there was one under the smokebox at the front on the running plate but this was impossible on the 0-6-2Ts, with their inside cylinders. H.C. Casserley, courtesy R.M. Casserley.

5665 at Barry shed, 6 July 1947, any emblem/lettering erased by weathering over the several years since the last repaint. No boiler grab irons or tank top lubricator (see 6658 in this section) but toolbox at front. The sliding shutter for once is in the 'closed' (a loose description!) position. H.C. Casserley, courtesy R.M. Casserley.

In green livery, 5669 stands at Cardiff Cathays shed in May 1927; it can't really be discerned here, but it carries GREAT WESTERN in serif on the tanks. Original taper buffers and oddly, it seems to have an extra 'spare' lamp bracket on the running plate. Good view of the covers of the inside steam chests for the eight inch diameter piston valves. ColourRail

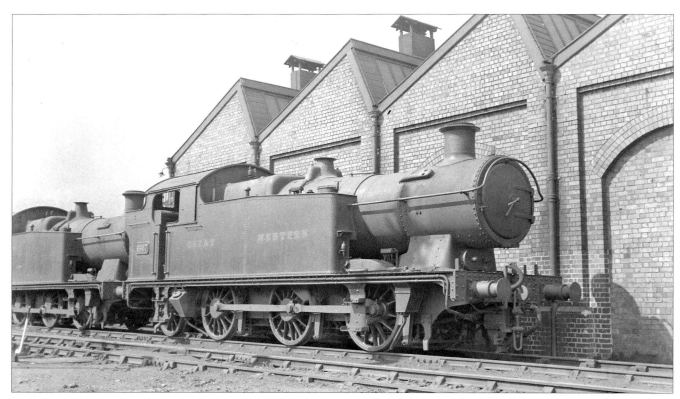

Serif GREAT WESTERN on ATC-fitted 6667 at Barry shed, 1930s. Smokebox overhang particularly obvious in this view. Parallel buffers. To repeat somewhat from earlier *Papers: The oil pipes to the cylinders and the Swindon design of smokebox-mounted regulator in the superheater header ran out of sight beneath the cladding but were not run through the front tubeplate but instead went outside the boiler barrel and then back in to the smokebox. All that takes place under the tapered cover on the right-hand side, where this piping briefly emerged (there were stopcocks under that dart-shaped cover, with leaks often present, streaking down the smokebox) to span boiler and smokebox. Most GW engines had hydrostatic sight feed displacement lubricators mounted in the cab, under the control of the driver. Increased/divided oil supply to valves and pistons meant there was a similar cover on the left-hand side of the smokebox on the tender engines but on most tanks it was concealed, underneath the boiler cladding.* The small upright bottle object on the front of the tank is the 'class B' vacuum pump lubricator. It supplied oil to the pump cylinder to lubricate the pump piston. ColourRail

6658 at Barry shed on 8 August 1954, quite late (if the date is correct) to still have the serif BRITISH RAILWAYS; livery would be green and – note – shiny bonnet and chimney cap. Route disc in conventional position above number plate. On top of the sloping part of the tank between the clack feeds by the bonnet and the tank filler is an oblong component. This is a lubricator, an oil tray with feeds running behind the tanks to the axleboxes. It was used on many of the 2-6-2Ts and 2-8-2Ts, but not the 2-8-0Ts. They are by no means universally present on the 0-6-2Ts but this might just reflect the amount of photographs we have to look at, and they were not always visible anyway, depending on the angle of the photograph. Following the pattern of the other classes, they were removed later on in some cases, replaced by something out of sight. ColourRail

5607 at Treherbert shed on 26 June 1938; lettering/emblem worn away in the years of hard work between Generals/ repaintings. No lamp recess 'wind shield' on bunker rear as yet. The bunker rear hand rails are centrally placed – on other locos they were lower, in line with the hand rail on the side of the bunker. See 5606 at Tyseley (page 25) for instance. No lubricator (see 6658 this section) on tank top; taper buffers. The 0-6-2Ts very rarely bore the stencilled GWR shed allocation codes on the running valence – too many rivets perhaps! The standard arrangement of through pipework on the 0-6-2Ts was steam heat right-hand side and vacuum brake pipe left-hand side – see also 5633 and 6694 (page 16, 18) in these *Introductory Notes*. Sometimes the left-hand vacuum piping ran behind the valence, however, as here, and was not visible. H.C. Casserley, courtesy R.M. Casserley.

5659 newly overhauled at Swindon; late 1950s/early 1960s. This is the arrangement of the right-hand piping, steam heat and usually lagged as here. Sometimes it was taken off if a loco was unlikely to work a passenger train in the winter. Clipped beneath, on the bottom edge of the valence, is the ATC conduit. So, should a loco have the left-hand side vacuum pipe hidden (as on 5607 above) and the right-hand side steam heat piping removed, it could be running with no pipes visible at all, either side. ColourRail

6602 with the Gill sans BRITISH RAILWAYS at Barry shed on 6 May 1951. The loco now has the prominent horizontal weld line on the tank, a response to corrosion in the lower part, and a standard 'mod' (modification) repair. Short bonnet, lubricator on tank top. H.C. Casserley, courtesy R.M. Casserley.

5601 at Abercynon on 16 October 1960, in final condition in black; it never got the lined green. Some repetition from earlier *Papers* is unavoidable in a series such as this, so here goes again: *On the right-hand side of some GWR classes (the majority of the GWR 4-cylinder and 2-outside cylinder tender locomotives in fact) there was a long, prominent pipe behind the hand rail, immediately in front of the right-hand cab window. This was the ejector, but the Manors, 2-6-0s and the tanks were different; the arrangement was internal, so there was no prominent pipe along the boiler behind the hand rail; it was made of copper, in contrast to the steel fire tubes.* ColourRail

5690 in a curious hybrid condition at Wolverhampton Stafford Road works, after repairs, on 10 June 1961. All trace of livery has gone, under grime or worn away while the front end, to which attention has been confined, is dazzling by comparison. Note the early half weld repair to the lower rear tank, the crudest seen by far. Lagged steam heat pipe on valence, clipped ATC conduit beneath. D. Forsyth, ColourRail

Outshopped at Swindon in glorious shimmering black, copper capped 6654 stands near the works turntable in 1954. The horizontal weld on the tank is lower than was often the case, preserving the integrity of the first, wheel and lion, emblem. The extra grab irons have appeared on the boiler side now; these found their way on to all the tanks, Prairies and eight-coupled, but seem to have come rather later so far as the 0-6-2Ts were concerned. Rail Photoprint.

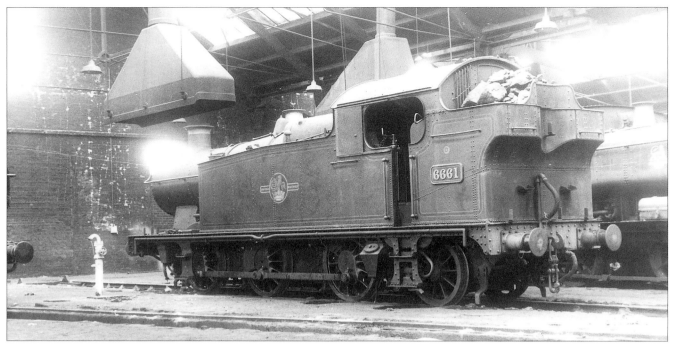

6661 at rest in the roundhouse at Aberdare, 13 July 1958; along with the lined green, acquired earlier in the year, it has received the new second emblem. No horizontal weld line suggests entirely new tanks, or second-hand replacements. Like the Big Prairies and eight coupled tanks (see *Papers* various) the 0-6-2Ts had a third water tank, under the coal space; the sloping line of rivets on the bunker marks the top of said water tank and the base of the bunker. This 'bunker tank' had to be connected to the two main side tanks and that square-section component like a wide 'U' behind the cab steps is the water levelling pipe; there will be another the other side. It was secured with a rubber joint between the rectangular mating surfaces and bolts which passed down from the inside of the tanks with fibre washers and nuts tightened against the pipe flanges. As recounted in earlier *Papers*: *These bolts frequently worked loose, causing leakage, and tightening them was difficult as the bolts tended to turn inside the tank. A regular job for an apprentice was to drop down into the tank through the filler hole and crawl along to the levelling pipe, to hold the bolt heads with a spanner while a fitter tightened the nuts on the outside. The bunker tank joint was not too difficult to work on as there was a removable plate which gave access to the joint.* H.C. Casserley, courtesy R.M. Casserley.

5633 with the second emblem but in black, at Treherbert on 29 August 1964. The water levelling pipe behind the cab steps, connecting the side tanks with the third tank under the coal space, described just now, was also employed in the eight-coupled tanks (see previous *Papers*) but they were prone to fracturing and had to be taken down to be welded, an unwieldy process in which the loco was unable to return to service until the pipe had been refitted and the tanks refilled. British Railways introduced an 'experimental armoured hose levelling pipe' in 1952 as a replacement, specifically for the 4200 and 7200 tanks and this was not visible from outside. There is no official record of its use being extended to the 0-6-2Ts but there are a number in which the pipe is absent, as on 5633 here. Presumably the 'experimental armoured pipe' has indeed been fitted – there had to be a levelling pipe somewhere of course, for the bunker tank had no separate filler. Michael Boakes Collection.

How the weld line ruined the emblem; 5617 at Swindon in black on 25 April 1954. Lubricator on tank top, no grab irons (though not all, apparently managed to get them), tank ventilator of later' flanged' type and a discreet bit of patchwork on the third water tank. The loco has acquired the toolbox at the front above the leading sand box. B. Griffiths, transporttreasury

5633 newly shopped, back home at Radyr MPD in 1963 in plain green; high weld line, tank top lubricator now gone, inevitable fire shovel on top, hitched to its retaining bracket by the cab window. The standard arrangement of through pipework on the 0-6-2Ts was steam heat (lagged, in theory) along the right-hand side running plate valence and vacuum brake pipe in the same position on the left-hand side. The vacuum pipe on 5633 here, on its left-hand side, can be identified by the small diameter pipe tee'd off the main pipe just under the front of the tank. This connected to the vacuum pump bolted to the inside face of the main frame. An individual engine might appear to carry one pipe, or both, or none, outside like this but they were still there, running on the inside of the valence. ColourRail

One of those with a toolbox, 5670 with BRITISH RAILWAYS in Gill sans comes through Birmingham Snow Hill about 1950. A splendidly jolting, banging, swaying, bumping, heterogeneous string of wooden PO wagons trailing behind. Michael Boakes Collection.

You wouldn't dare to model it 1. 'Shirt button' emblem gone walkabout on 6694. Here we have the right-hand side and (referring back to 5633) the pipework along the valence of the running plate this time carries the steam heat, though it is not lagged as (ideally) it should be. The fact is, a number of the class working from sheds in South Wales had their steam heating equipment isolated as they were employed mainly on coal operations, so lagging went by the by. These could be identified by the absence of the buffer beam control cock, the pipe being left open ended. In some cases, the entire run of steam heat piping might be removed. transporttreasury

You wouldn't dare to model it 2. '628' (it's actually 6628) rumbles around the sidings at Swansea Victoria, 4 August 1962. transporttreasury

You wouldn't dare to model it 3. A fine view of two 0-6-2Ts outside Cardiff Cathays MPD on 31 August 1956. The aspect you wouldn't think to model is the doubling up of front top lamp irons on 5654. The chance juxtaposition of new smokebox doors was the cause and up to thirty are known to have run thus. transporttreasury

5600 Allocation by Richard Derry

5600 Cathays 15/12/24; Cardiff Docks 25/1/25; Barry 22/2/25; Cathays 5/9/26; Barry 26/12/26; Cathays 15/5/27; Barry 12/6/27; Croes Newydd 14/11/36; Merthyr 12/12/36; Treherbert 9/1/37; Barry 2/42; Treherbert 10/42; Cathays 4/23/54; Treherbert 16/7/55; Radyr 29/1/55; Treherbert 13/8/55; **w/d 27/7/62; sold to J Cashmore, Newport 18/9/62; mileage 684,080**

5601 Cardiff Docks 29/12/24; Rhymney 14/6/25; Cae Harris 26/10/28; Treherbert 30/8/30; Cathays 2/7/32; Treherbert 30/7/32**;** Abercynon 24/6/39; Treherbert 22/7/39; Barry 3/41; Treherbert 4/41; Cathays 3/45; Treherbert 4/45; Cathays 15/6/46; Treherbert 13/7/46; Cathays 22/2/47; Treherbert 22/3/47; Cathays 23/4/49; Abercynon 30/11/57; Rhymney 28/11/64; **w/d 15/1/65; sold to J E Woodfield, Newport 1/3/65; mileage at 28/12/63 823,488**

5602 Cardiff Docks 1/1/25; Barry 22/3/25; Newport Ebbw Jct 12/12/36; Aberdare 1/43; Newport Ebbw Jct 2/43; Pontypool Road 11/8/51; Aberbeeg 17/5/52; Cardiff Canton 27/3/54; Llanelly 13/8/60; Swansea East Dock 27/7/63; Rhymney 30/11/63; Merthyr 13/6/64; Radyr 12/7/64; **w/d 9/64; cut up, no date; mileage at 28/12/63 669,357**

5603 Cardiff Docks 12/1/25; Trehafod 22/2/25; Cathays 14/6/25; Barry 1/11/25; Cathays 5/9/26; Barry 26/12/25; Merthyr 30/9/28; Newport Ebbw Jct 15/3/30; Aberbeeg 10/5/30; Newport Ebbw Jct 29/8/31; Aberbeeg 26/9/31; Newport Ebbw Jct 27/8/32; Aberbeeg 24/9/32; Newport Ebbw Jct 22/10/32; Aberbeeg 21/9/35; Newport Ebbw Jct 19/10/35; Newport Pill 26/2/49; Newport Ebbw Jct 18/6/49; Swansea East Dock 16/7/49; Neath 8/10/49; Cardiff East Dock 3/12/49; Merthyr 20/5/50; **w/d 9/64; sold to R S Hayes, Bridgend 27/10/64; mileage at 28/12/63 765,862**

5604 Cardiff Docks 17/1/25; Trehafod 22/2/25; Treherbert 1/11/25; Landore 16/11/35; Tondu 5/3/38; Landore 20/8/38; Treherbert 15/10/38; Landore 10/12/38; Duffryn Yard 14/6/58; Llanelly 9/9/61; **w/d 13/12/62; sold to R S Hayes, Bridgend 26/8/63; mileage 50,560**

5605 Barry 27/1/25; Carmarthen 5/42; Cathays 11/43; Merthyr 4/45; Cathays 5/45; Treherbert 7/45; Cathays 9/45; Merthyr 17/4/48; Cathays 15/5/48; Newport Ebbw Jct 21/5/49; Merthyr 3/12/49; Abercynon 16/5/64; Rhymney 28/11/64; Tyseley 22/5/65; Croes Newydd 1/1/66; **w/d 5/66; mileage at 28/12/63 765,754**

5606 Trehafod 12/2/25; Coke Ovens 14/6/25; Cathays 9/8/25; Trehafod 4/10/25; Treherbert 1/11/25; Cathays 25/12/27; Ferndale 25/11/28; Cathays 6/4/35; Ferndale 4/5/35; Severn Tunnel Jct 2/5/36; Duffryn Yard 17/10/36; Oxley 15/6/47; Stourbridge 4/11/50; Tyseley 6/9/58; Wrexham Rhosddu 27/12/58; Croes Newydd 30/1/60; Oxley 10/9/60; Tyseley 21/3/64; **w/d 13/11/65**

5607 Trehafod 11/2/25; Treherbert1/11/25; Ferndale 2/10/27; Treherbert 27/11/27; Cathays 1933; Treherbert 13/1/34; Cathays 6/2/37; Treherbert 6/3/37; Cathays 21/8/37; Treherbert 18/9/37; Cathays 10/12/38; Treherbert 7/1/39; Cathays 11/45; Merthyr 29/12/45; Treherbert 18/5/46; Cardiff East Dock 10/8/46; Treherbert 7/9/46; Barry 29/11/47; Treherbert 27/12/47; **w/d 16/12/63; cut up 25/1/64; mileage 867,463**

5608 Abercynon 14/2/25; Treherbert 1/11/25; Cathays 28/6/35; Treherbert 27/7/35; Cathays 1/5/37; Treherbert 29/5/37; Cathays 10/12/38; Treherbert 10/42; Barry 6/44; Treherbert 6/44; Barry 12/44; Abercynon 20/4/46; Treherbert 18/5/46; Cathays 16/7/55; Radyr 29/1/55; Treherbert 13/8/55; **w/d 29/8/63; sold to R S Hayes, Bridgend 1/1/64; mileage 757,936**

5609 Barry 18/2/25; Cathays 7/7/29; Barry 4/8/29; Landore 1933; Danygraig 30/6/34; Landore 25/8/34; Duffryn Yard 17/11/34; Aberdare 9/2/35; Barry 4/40; Cathays 10/45; Barry 25/1/47; Swansea East Dock 10/9/59; Merthyr 28/12/63; **w/d 19/10/64; sold to R S Hayes, Bridgend 10/12/64; mileage at 28/12/63 764,735**

5610 Barry 20/2/25; Cathays 5/9/26; Barry 26/12/25; Treherbert 9/1/37; Merthyr 8/42; Barry 11/42; Cardiff East Dock 6/45; Treherbert 7/45; Barry 6/9/47; Treherbert 29/11/47; Cathays 4/12/54; Treherbert 16/7/55; Duffryn Yard 28/11/59; Merthyr 26/12/59; **w/d 16/12/63; sold to Birds Ltd, Morriston 28/2/64; mileage 724,605**

5611 Cathays 2/3/25; Cae Harris 12/7/25; Treherbert 30/8/30; Cathays 24/8/35; Treherbert 3/41; Cardiff East Dock 4/41; Treherbert 5/41; Cathays 3/43; Treherbert 6/43; Cathays 5/10/46; Treherbert 2/11/46; Cathays 2/10/48; Treherbert 30/10/48; **w/d 9/1/63; sold to J Cashmore, Newport 6/63; mileage 806,691**

5612 Cathays 2/3/25; Cae Harris 14/6/25; Cathays 12/7/25; Cardiff Docks 9/8/25; Cae Harris 6/9/25; Newport Ebbw Jct 16/11/35; Barry 24/7/37; Newport Ebbw Jct 21/8/37; Cathays 12/41; Barry 3/42; Carmarthen 5/42; Duffryn Yard 4/43; Swansea Victoria 11/8/51; Llanelly 28/11/53; **w/d 23/4/63; sold to J Cashmore, Newport 7/11/63; mileage 580,615**

5613 Cathays 3/3/25; Cae Harris 14/6/25; Cathays 26/12/25; Cardiff Docks 23/12/28; Cae Harris 1/9/29; Cathays 18/1/30; Cae Harris 15/3/30; Swansea East Dock 16/11/35; Abercynon 8/1/38; Newport Ebbw Jct 5/2/38; Abercynon 23/7/38; Newport Ebbw Jct 20/8/38; Abercynon 10/12/38; Pantyffynon 8/1/38; Radyr 4/43; Treherbert 12/43; Barry 6/9/47; Treherbert 4/10/47; Cardiff East Dock 15/5/48; Treherbert 10/7/48; Radyr 14/7/62; **w/d 7/5/65; sold to Birds, Morriston 16/6/65; mileage at 28/12/63 691,445**

An 0-6-2T in the heart of England, at Tyseley, in 1965 when the ranks of the locos were getting thin indeed. 5606 has acquired (and lost) an electrification flash by dint of being based at what by now is an LMR MPD. In the months before it was withdrawn, at the end of 1965, for the first time there were more 0-6-2Ts (we are talking remnants only of course) in England than in Wales! Rail Online

5608 gets its train of coal away at Ferndale, on 16 August 1957. R. Broughton, ColourRail

5640 Cathays 29/10/25; Barry 29/11/25; Treherbert 21/3/26; Cathays 24/11/29; Treherbert 22/12/29; Abercynon 24/6/39; Treherbert 16/9/39; Cathays 6/1/40; Barry 3/41; Cathays 4/41; Merthyr 1/43; Cathays 3/43; Barry 9/44; Cathays 10/44; Merthyr 3/11/45; Cathays 18/5/46; Radyr 30/11/46; Merthyr 3/11/51; Radyr 21/1/59; St Philips Marsh 10/9/60; Leamington Spa 8/9/62; **w/d 6/6/63; sold to J Cashmore, Great Bridge 17/10/63; mileage 747,287**

5641 Coke Ovens 5/11/25; Abercynon 10/3/34; Cathays 18/9/37; Abercynon 16/10/37; Barry 11/11/39; Abercynon 9/12/39; Cathays 2/41; Abercynon 3/41; Barry 9/42; Abercynon 10/42; Barry 12/42; Abercynon 29/12/45; Merthyr 12/7/47; Abercynon 9/8/47; **w/d 7/9/64; sold to J Cashmore, Newport 14/10/64; mileage at 28/12/63 806,353**

5642 Cathays 31/10/25; Coke Ovens 29/11/25; Abercynon 13/1/34; Newport Ebbw Jct 12/12/36; Cathays 26/6/38; Newport Ebbw Jct 23/7/38; Barry 4/40; Treherbert 6/42; Shrewsbury 11/42; Stourbridge 1/11/52; Cardiff East Dock 30/1/54; Gloucester 16/7/55; Didcot 11/9/55; St Philips Marsh 6/11/55; Aberdare 13/6/59; **w/d 21/9/62; cut up 23/2/63 at Caerphilly Works; mileage 622,475**

5643 Cathays 29/11/25; Coke Ovens 26/12/26; Abercynon 24/10/31; Cardiff Docks 21/11/31; Coke Ovens 19/12/31; Abercynon 1933; Cathays 6/3/37; Abercynon 29/5/37; Barry 6/1/40; Abercynon 3/2/40; Barry 30/3/40; Abercynon 4/40; Cathays 8/40; Abercynon 9/40; Merthyr 3/42; Cathays 8/42; Cardiff East Dock 10/42; Abercynon 12/42; Cardiff East Dock 8/45; Abercynon 9/45; Cardiff East Dock 10/45; Abercynon 11/45; Cathays 10/8/46; Abercynon 7/9/46; Cathays 5/10/46; Abercynon 2/11/46; Barry 17/6/61; **w/d 6/6/63; sold to J Cashmore, Great Bridge 17/10/63; mileage 776,993**

5644 Cathays 6/11/25; Coke Ovens 26/12/26; Cathays 13/1/34; Abercynon 10/2/34; Cathays 11/1/36; Abercynon 8/2/36; Merthyr 10/44; Abercynon 11/44; Treherbert 6/45; Abercynon 9/45; Cathays 23/2/46; Abercynon 23/3/46; Treherbert 10/9/48; Abercynon 27/11/48; Aberdare 5/9/53; Abercynon 17/5/58; **w/d 17/6/63; cut up 7/9/63; mileage 742,989**

5645 Cathays 13/11/25; Ferndale 26/12/26; Severn Tunnel Jct 28/7/34; Newport Ebbw Jct 24/8/35; Severn Tunnel Jct 19/10/35; Newport Ebbw Jct 3/2/40; Severn Tunnel Jct 2/3/40; Merthyr 8/45; Cathays 9/45; Severn Tunnel Jct 18/1/47; Aberbeeg 31/10/53;Pontypool Road 25/1/58; Merthyr 19/5/62; **w/d 7/6/63; cut up 22/2/64; mileage 576,973**

5646 Cathays 17/11/25; Barry 27/12/25; Treherbert 21/3/26; Ferndale 29/8/31; Cathays 21/11/31; Treherbert 19/12/31; Ferndale 17/10/36; Treherbert 14/11/36; Cathays 6/1/40; Merthyr 8/40; Cathays 9/40; Newport Ebbw Jct 8/41; Severn Tunnel Jct 4/43; Newport Ebbw Jct 10/43; Merthyr 11/43; Cathays 12/43; Treherbert 7/9/46; Cathays 5/10/46; Duffryn Yard 16/7/49; Swansea Victoria 11/8/51; Whitland 26/1/52; Treherbert 9/10/55; **w/d 1/9/62; sold to R S Hayes, Bridgend 26/8/63; mileage 728,719**

5647 Cathays 14/11/25; Coke Ovens 24/1/26; Cae Harris 23/12/28; Cathays 15/12/34; Treherbert 6/2/37; Chester 11/42; Stafford Road 10/45; Chester 11/45; Oxley 24/1/48; Chester 21/2/48; Didcot 1/12/56; Abercynon 13/8/60; Aberdare 8/9/62; **w/d 10/3/64; sold to Barborough Metals, Chesterfield 19/3/64; mileage at 28/12/63 622,285**

5648 Cathays 20/11/25; Ferndale 26/12/26; Cathays 26/12/29; Ferndale 14/2/31; Duffryn Yard 2/5/36; Swansea East Dock 2/3/40; Duffryn Yard 7/40; Cathays 4/43; Barry 6/43; Cathays 19/4/47; Merthyr 25/1/47; Barry 17/5/47; Cardiff East Dock 5/10/57; Radyr 22/3/58; **w/d 5/10/64; sold to R S Hayes, Bridgend 27/10/64; mileage at 28/12/63 717,521**

5649 Cathays 23/11/25 Radyr 26/12/26; Cathays 10/7/27; Radyr 4/9/27; Cathays 5/8/28; Radyr 2/9/28; Cae Harris 24/11/29; Pontypool Road 28/7/34; Newport Ebbw Jct 21/8/37; Pontypool Road 18/9/37; Aberdare 30/10/48; **w/d 15/3/63; sold to J Cashmore, Newport 7/11/63; mileage 611,406**

5650 Cathays 26/1/26; Abercynon 21/3/26; Cathays 18/4/26; Rhymney 8/8/26; Cathays 5/9/26; Radyr 26/12/26; Abercynon 20/3/27; Coke Ovens 15/5/27; Cathays 22/12/29; Coke Ovens 18/1/30; Landore 1933; Abercynon 4/43; Treherbert 5/45; Barry 11/45; Treherbert 1/12/45; Cathays 20/3/48; Treherbert 17/4/48; Abercynon 31/12/49; Cathays 6/9/52; Merthyr 9/10/55; **w/d 24/6/63; sold to R S Hayes, Bridgend 1/1/64; mileage 767,030**

5651 Cathays 26/1/26; Radyr 26/12/26; Cathays 17/4/27; Radyr 15/5/27; Cathays 7/8/27; Radyr 2/10/27; Cathays 30/10/27; Radyr 27/11/27; Treherbert 18/3/28; Radyr 13/5/28; Cathays 25/11/28; Radyr 15/3/30; Cathays 17/1/31; Radyr 14/2/31; Cathays 19/12/31; Radyr 16/1/32; Cathays 1933; Abercynon 9/2/35; Cathays 9/3/35; Cardiff East Dock 2/41; Cathays 3/41; Radyr 12/41; Cathays 5/42; Barry 1/43; Cathays 5/43; Merthyr 8/43; Cathays 10/43; Merthyr 14/6/46; Cathays 12/7/46; Stourbridge 23/4/49; Worcester 7/9/57; Tyseley 5/10/57; Shrewsbury 1/11/58; Wrexham Rhosddu 27/12/58; Croes Newydd 30/1/60; Radyr 29/12/62; Merthyr 20/4/63; Rhymney 28/11/64; **w/d 26/12/64; sold to Woodham Brothers, Barry 11/2/65; mileage at 28/12/63 643,085**

5652 Cathays 1/2/26; Rhymney 26/12/26; Cathays 25/11/28; Radyr 20/12/29; Cathays 27/10/29; Radyr 24/11/29; Cae Harris 22/12/29; Cardiff East Dock 29/6/35; Cae Harris 21/9/35; Cathays 30/5/36; Cae Harris 27/6/36; Merthyr 28/5/38; Barry 6/42; Merthyr 12/42; Cathays 6/43; Merthyr 2/44; Cathays 9/44; Merthyr 12/44; Radyr 12/7/47; Cathays 9/8/47; Merthyr 20/3/48; **w/d 27/9/62; cut up 26/1/63 at Caerphilly Works; mileage 675,454**

5611 runs into Radyr station in the rain, with the 10.23am Cardiff-Merthyr, on 5 May 1951. H.C. Casserley, courtesy R.M. Casserley.

5613 with toolbox, under the overly-commodious coaling shelter at Ferndale shed in 1963. For years the little shed here was an outstation (later 'sub-shed') of Treherbert though it was reportedly placed under Radyr instead from June 1962. 5613 here has the 88F plate of Treherbert, over the hill to the west, in the Rhondda though at other times the odd couple of 0-6-2Ts to be found stabled at Ferndale would come from Radyr — on 7 April 1964 for instance, when Radyr's 6606 and 6626 were noted. D.K. Jones Collection.

5653 Cathays 5/2/26; Cae Harris 26/12/26; Merthyr 27/6/36; Cathays 25/7/36; Cae Harris 14/11/36; Merthyr 5/41; Cathays 8/43; Barry 4/10/47; Merthyr 1/11/47; Cathays 7/10/50; Treherbert 28/12/57; Barry 14/7/62; **w/d 1/1/63; sold to J Cashmore, Newport 18/6/63; mileage 701,355**

5654 Cathays 9/2/26; Rhymney 15/5/26; Cae Harris 11/7/26; Barry 7/7/29; Cae Harris 4/8/29; Barry 22/10/32; Cae Harris 1933; Merthyr 1/6/35; Cae Harris 29/6/35; Merthyr 19/10/35; Cae Harris 16/11/35; Barry 17/10/36; Rhymney 14/11/36; Cathays 18/9/37; Cae Harris 16/10/37; Rhymney 13/11/37; Cae Harris 11/12/37; Barry 2/41; Treherbert 3/41; Merthyr 4/41; Barry 12/41; Merthyr 1/42; Cathays 10/42; Merthyr 11/42; Cathays 22/2/47; Merthyr 22/3/47; Cathays 7/10/50; Treherbert 28/12/57; Radyr 14/7/62; **w/d 16/12/63; sold to Birds, Morriston 28/2/64; mileage 751,918**

5655 Cathays 2/2/26; Rhymney 26/12/26; Dowlais Central 25/12/27; Rhymney 19/2/28; Dowlais Central 5/5/34; Rhymney 2/6/34; Merthyr 30/4/38; Cardiff East Dock 12/41; Merthyr 1/42; Barry 12/42; Merthyr 2/43; Cathays 8/43; Merthyr 11/43; Merthyr 1/44; Cathays 2/44; Cardiff East Dock 9/44; Merthyr 10/44; Abercynon 1/12/45; Cathays 12/7/46; Abercynon 6/9/46; Radyr 29/11/46; Cathays 6/9/47; Radyr 1/11/47; Merthyr 20/3/48; Barry 4/9/48; Radyr 2/10/48; Merthyr 15/7/50; Rhymney 28/11/64; **w/d 3/6/65; sold to T W Ward, Briton Ferry 28/7/65; mileage at 28/12/63 810,205**

5656 Cathays 11/2/26; Rhymney 26/12/26; Dowlais Central 20/2/27; Rhymney 20/3/27; Neath 28/7/34; Duffryn Yard 19/10/35; Landore 17/4/48; Neath 13/6/59; Llanelly 26/12/60; Swansea East Dock 8/9/62; Llanelly 31/12/63; **w/d 14/2/64; sold to R S Hayes Bridgend 2/4/64; mileage at 28/12/63 631,266**

5657 Cathays 9/2/26; Penarth Dock 15/4/28; Barry 12/5/28; Abercynon 18/1/30; Landore 28/7/34; Neath 20/10/34; Danygraig 17/11/34; Swansea East Dock 8/45; Oxley 12/7/47; Whitland 12/7/52; Llanelly 4/10/52; Oxley 1/11/52; Llanelly 29/11/52; Swansea Victoria 8/8/53; Llanelly 31/10/53; Newport Ebbw Jct 4/12/55; Aberbeeg 2/11/57; Newport Ebbw Jct 30/11/57; Abercynon 19/5/62; **w/d 27/7/62; sold to J Cashmore, Newport 18/9/62; mileage 540,562**

5658 Cathays 10/2/26; Radyr 19/2/28; Coke |Ovens 27/12/28; Radyr 15/2/30; Cathays 7/6/30; Radyr 5/7/30; Cathays 20/12/30; Radyr 17/1/31; Cathays 1933; Abercynon 2/41; Cathays 3/41; Merthyr 12/41; Treherbert 1/42; Cathays 2/42; Merthyr 8/42; Cathays 10/42; Merthyr 8/45; Treherbert 9/45; Cathays 10/45; Barry 27/12/46; Cathays 25/1/47; Stourbridge 23/4/49; Tyseley 6/9/58; Leamington Spa 1/12/62; Tyseley 23/2/64; **w/d 13/11/65**

5659 Cathays 18/2/26; Radyr 20/3/27; Cathays 15/5/27; Radyr 10/7/27; Cathays 28/10/28; Radyr 25/11/28; Cae Harris 12/5/29; Cathays 25/10/30; Treherbert 22/11/30; Cathays 12/1/35; Treherbert 9/2/35; Barry 14/12/35; Cathays 18/9/37; Treherbert 16/10/37; Merthyr 4/43; Cathays 7/43; Barry 10/45; Merthyr 11/45; Cathays 28/12/46; Merthyr 7/10/50; Cathays 3/11/51; Radyr 21/2/53; Pontypool Road 16/7/55; Treherbert 18/4/64; Merthyr 13/6/64; Rhymney 28/11/64; Stourbridge 24/4/65; Croes Newydd 6/11/65; **w/d 27/11/65; mileage at 28/12/63 750,562**

5660 Cathays 19/2/26; Radyr 23/12/27; Cathays 20/2/27; Treherbert 30/10/27; Cathays 27/11/27; Rhymney 19/2/28; Cardiff Docks 24/11/29; Rhymney 22/12/29; Cae Harris 16/10/37; Rhymney 11/12/37; Merthyr 3/41; Cathays 8/41; Barry 11/41; Merthyr 12/41; Cardiff East Dock 12/42; Merthyr 1/43; Barry 14/6/46; Merthyr 12/7/46; Abercynon 5/9/53; Merthyr 30/1/54; Radyr 5/9/64; **w/d 23/10/64; sold to R S Hayes, Bridgend 10/12/64; mileage at 28/12/63 859,732**

5661 Cathays 23/2/26; Rhymney 13/6/26; Cathays 8/8/26; Radyr 12/6/27; Cathays 10/7/27; Radyr 30/10/27; Cathays 27/11/27; Rhymney 19/2/28; Barry 9/6/29; Rhymney 7/7/29; Severn Tunnel Jct 14/3/31; Merthyr 24/10/31; Cathays 9/2/35; Merthyr 6/4/35; Cathays 12/12/36; Merthyr 1/5/37; Cae Harris 26/6/37; Merthyr 24/7/37; Cathays 1/42; Treherbert 5/44; Cathays 6/44; Merthyr 6/10/45; Treherbert 1/12/45; Cathays 29/12/45; Treherbert 25/1/47; Cathays 22/3/47; Barry 17/5/47; Merthyr 14/6/47; Cathays 9/8/47; Whitland 17/6/50; Merthyr 19/5/51; **w/d 27/7/62; sold to J Cashmore, Newport 18/9/62; mileage 768,161**

5662 Abercynon 25/2/26; Aberdare 24/11/29; Landore 28/7/34; Barry 5/43; Merthyr 5/45; Barry 6/45; Merthyr 2/10/48; **w/d 13/11/64; sold to R S Hayes, Bridgend 12/1/65; mileage at 28/12/63 737,312**

5663 Cathays 15/3/26; Penarth Dock 25/12/27; Barry 19/2/28; Treherbert 28/10/28; Swansea East Dock 28/7/34; Neath 17/10/36; Treherbert 4/43; Cathays 7/45; Treherbert 8/45; Barry 29/12/45; Treherbert 25/1/47; Cathays 29/11/47; Treherbert 27/12/47; Cathays 24/1/48; Treherbert 21/2/48; Barry 7/8/48 Treherbert 27/11/48; Barry 8/9/51; Cathays 31/10/53; Treherbert 28/12/57; Radyr 21/2/59; **w/d 3/8/62; sold to J Cashmore, Newport 18/9/62; mileage 699,569**

5664 Cathays 5/3/26; Radyr 30/10/27; Barry 25/12/27; Cathays 8/41; Barry 9/41; Radyr 6/9/47; Barry 27/12/47; **w/d 31/8/62; cut up 18/7/63; mileage 682,825**

5665 Cathays 12/6/26; Treherbert 28/11/26; Cathays 26/12/26; Treherbert 18/3/28; Radyr 15/4/28; Coke Ovens 30/9/28; Radyr 28/10/28; Treherbert 22/12/29; Merthyr 5/43; Barry 9/43; Merthyr 7/8/48; Cathays 4/9/48; Barry 27/11/48; Treherbert 9/10/55; Pontypool Road 27/3/65; **w/d 16/6/65; sold to T W Ward, Briton Ferry 28/7/65; mileage at 757,882**

5666 Cathays 11/6/26; Coke Ovens 3/10/26; Cathays 26/12/26; Coke Ovens 25/12/27; Barry 19/2/28; Cathays 29/6/35; Merthyr 3/41; Cathays 4/41; Merthyr 12/41; Barry 1/42; Merthyr 2/42; Barry 10/43; Merthyr 11/43; Cathays 1/11/46; Merthyr 29/11/46; Barry 2/10/48; Cathays 30/10/48; Merthyr 21/4/50; Cardiff East Dock 23/3/57; Merthyr 18/5/57; **w/d 16/7/63; sold to J Cashmore, Newport 7/11/63; mileage 714,708**

5616 smart in newly-applied lined green, polished cap and bonnet, at Canton – around 1958 at a guess. Two top front lamp irons, tank top lubricator; engine still has taper buffers. ColourRail

Toolbox-fitted 5617, in lined green and with water levelling pipe behind footsteps prominent, at Abercynon on 16 October 1960. The trailing axle was radial, as with all large WR tanks. RailOnline

5667 Cathays 18/6/26; Coke Ovens 31/10/26; Radyr 26/12/26; Cathays 23/1/27; Radyr 15/5/27; Cathays 12/6/27; Radyr 2/10/27; Cae Harris 28/10/28; Rhymney 1/9/29; Cae Harris 29/9/29; Ferndale 1933; Duffryn Yard 2/5/36; Stafford Road 10/12/38; Carmarthen 5/42; Barry 7/43; Merthyr 9/44; Barry 2/45; Croes Newydd 8/8/63; **w/d 17/7/65**

5668 Cathays 23/6/26; Coke Ovens 31/10/26; Cathays 26/12/26; Barry 25/11/28; Cae Harris 22/12/29; Merthyr 25/7/36; Cae Harris 22/8/36; Merthyr 21/8/37; Cae Harris 16/10/37; Treherbert 20/8/38; Barry 10/43; Treherbert 11/43; Cathays 1/45; Treherbert 2/45; Cardiff East Dock 22/2/46; Treherbert 22/3/46; Cathays 24/3/51; Treherbert 11/8/51; Barry 17/6/61; **w/d 7/9/65; sold to Woodham Brothers, Barry 14/10/64; mileage at 28/12/63 762,424; engine preserved**

5669 Cathays 2/7/26; Treherbert 31/10/26; Cathays 26/12/26; Coke Ovens 28/10/28; Cathays 10/5/30; Coke Ovens 7/6/30; Abercynon 13/1/34; Cardiff East Dock 12/41; Abercynon 1/42; Cathays 2/45; Abercynon 3/45; Cardiff East Dock 9/45; Abercynon 10/45; Barry 1/11/47; Cathays 21/2/48; Abercynon 20/3/48; Cathays 23/4/49; Radyr 28/12/57; Treherbert 4/10/58;Radyr 1/11/58; Treherbert 26/1/63; Radyr 16/5/64; **w/d 7/9/64; sold to Woodham Brothers, Barry 14/10/64; mileage at 28/12/63 786,835**

5670 Newport Ebbw Jct 19/8/26; Aberbeeg 4/8/29; Newport Ebbw Jct 29/9/29; Cardiff Canton 30/8/30; Newport Ebbw Jct 17/11/34; Cardiff Canton 15/12/34; Newport Ebbw Jct 2/4/38; Cardiff Canton 30/4/38; Cathays 23/7/38; Cardiff Canton 20/8/38; Neath 9/42; Oxley 17/5/47; Cathays 23/4/49; Radyr 28/12/57; Merthyr 17/5/58; Duffryn Yard 26/12/59; Merthyr 28/12/63; **w/d 19/10/64; sold to R S Hayes, Bridgend 10/12/64; mileage at 28/12/63 795,479**

5671 Newport Ebbw Jct 16/8/26; Bassaleg 23/12/28; Newport Ebbw Jct 14/4/29; Cardiff Canton 24/11/29; Newport Ebbw Jct 15/3/30; Merthyr 12/4/30; Cardiff Canton 7/5/32; Merthyr 4/6/32; Cardiff Cathays 29/6/35; Merthyr 19/10/35; Cae Harris 11/1/36; Merthyr 8/2/36; Cae Harris 7/3/36; Merthyr 2/5/36; Cardiff East Dock 22/8/36; Merthyr 9/1/37; Cae Harris 13/11/37; Merthyr 11/12/37; Barry 14/6/47; Merthyr 9/8/47; Abercynon 25/12/48; Merthyr 29/1/49; Treherbert 11/7/53; Merthyr 8/8/53; **w/d 6/1/64; cut up 21/3/64; mileage at 28/12/63 775,804**

5672 Newport Ebbw Jct 17/8/26; Merthyr 25/12/27; Cae Harris 24/8/35; Cathays 14/12/35; Merthyr 11/1/36; Cae Harris 26/6/37; Merthyr 16/10/37; Barry 5/42; Merthyr 6/42; Barry 4/44; Cathays 5/44; Treherbert 13/7/46; Cathays 10/8/46; Barry 2/11/46; Cathays 30/11/46; Treherbert 21/2/48; Merthyr 20/3/48; Radyr 1/12/62; **w/d 13/9/63; sold to R S Hayes, Bridgend 1/1/64; mileage at 28/12/63 764,343**

5673 Newport Ebbw Jct 25/8/26; Bassaleg 30/9/28; Newport Ebbw Jct 17/3/29; Aberbeeg 24/11/29; Newport Ebbw Jct 22/12/29; Stafford Road 13/1/34; Leamington Spa 2/6/34; Stafford Road 16/11/35; Leamington Spa 14/12/35; Shrewsbury 19/9/36; Whitland 14/6/52; Swansea Victoria 6/9/52; Landore 4/10/52; Neath 17/6/61; Radyr 5/9/63; **w/d 8/3/65; sold to Birds, Bynea 8/4/65; mileage at 28/12/63 538,177**

5674 Treherbert 10/9/26; Coke Ovens 6/6/31; Cae Harris 26/6/37; Abercynon 24/7/37; Barry 12/41; Merthyr 2/42; Cardiff East Dock 10/43; Merthyr 11/43; Barry 11/45; Merthyr 1/12/45; Treherbert 7/10/61; **w/d 20/4/64; sold to Birds, Morriston 3/6/64; mileage at 28/12/63 737,704**

5675 Coke Ovens 13/9/26; Llanelly 28/7/34; Cathays 3/41; Treherbert 4/41; Llanelly 30/11/46; Pantyffynon 14/6/47; Landore 29/1/49; Llanelly 1/5/49; Swansea Victoria 21/4/51; Llanelly 19/5/51; Swansea Victoria 24/1/53; Llanelly 21/2/53; St Philips Marsh 5/9/53; Didcot 4/12/55; Reading 17/5/58; Radyr 21/1/59; Swansea East Dock 5/9/59; Llanelly 13/6/63; **w/d 26/12/64; sold to G Cohen, Morriston 11/2/65; mileage at 28/12/63 593,776**

5676 Cathays 10/9/26; Radyr 17/4/27; Cathays 15/5/27; Radyr 10/7/27; Cathays 4/9/27; Barry 25/12/27; Treherbert 28/10/28; Cathays 27/9/30; Treherbert 25/10/30; Ferndale 12/3/32; Treherbert 9/4/32; Treherbert 9/4/32; Cathays 10/11/36; Treherbert 12/12/36; Barry 5/44; Treherbert 6/44; Cathays 11/44; Treherbert 12/44; Cathays 10/45; Treherbert 11/45; Cardiff East Dock 1/12/45; Treherbert 29/12/45; Cardiff East Dock 15/6/46; Treherbert 28/12/46; Radyr 16/5/64; Croes Newydd 5/9/64; **w/d 6/11/65; mileage at 28/12/63 827,313**

5677 Cardiff Canton 16/9/26; Severn Tunnel Jct 30/10/27; Merthyr 15/2/30; Cathays 22/10/32; Merthyr 19/11/32; Merthyr 2/41; Cathays 9/41; Merthyr 10/41; Barry 8/42; Merthyr 9/42; Cardiff East Dock 4/45; Merthyr 5/45; Cathays 7/45; Merthyr 8/45; Cathays 7/9/46; Merthyr 2/11/46; Cathays 27/2/54; Merthyr 6/10/56; Neath 6/10/62; Merthyr 29/12/62; Rhymney 28/11/64; Croes Newydd 24/4/65; **w/d 6/11/65; mileage at 28/12/63 893,451**

5678 Cardiff Canton 17/9/26; Severn Tunnel Jct 30/10/27; Newport Ebbw Jct 17/2/29; Aberbeeg 12/5/29; Newport Ebbw Jct 1/9/29; Aberbeeg 29/9/29; Newport Ebbw Jct 15/2/30; Aberbeeg 5/7/30; Merthyr 25/10/30; Cathays 16/11/35; Merthyr 14/12/35; Cathays 30/5/36; Merthyr 22/8/36; Cae Harris 19/9/36; Merthyr 17/10/36; Cae Harris 1/5/37; Merthyr 26/6/37; Cathays 6/4/45; Merthyr 7/45; Radyr 15/7/50; Treherbert 23/2/57; **w/d 15/1/64; sold to T W Ward, Briton Ferry 24/3/64; mileage at 28/12/63 863,145**

5679 Cardiff Canton 16/10/26; Merthyr 25/12/27; Cardiff Canton 30/9/28; Newport Ebbw Jct 6/3/37; Cardiff Canton 3/4/37; Newport Ebbw Jct 1/5/37; Cardiff Canton 29/5/37; Barry 2/44; Cardiff Canton 3/44; Severn Tunnel Jct 21/2/59; Pontypool Road 28/11/59; Croes Newydd 21/4/62; Barry 29/1/62; Croes Newydd 23/2/63; Stourbridge 20/4/63; **w/d 29/7/63; cut up 5/10/63; mileage 709,991**

5618 approaching Cowbridge Road Crossing, near Llantrisant, on 3 May 1958. The curious loads behind the engine are two loose tanks, roped into open wagons; the train, Target X2, is not an over-long one but nevertheless a pannier tank, 3617, is assisting at the rear. S. Rickard J&J Collection, D.K. Jones.

A scruffy 5621, front number plate gone, alongside another 0-6-2T with empties, at remaining steam pocket Nelson, in 1964. Safety valves visible above bonnet. Michael Boakes Collection.

5680 Barry 11/10/26; Treherbert 28/10/28; Cardiff Docks 29/2/29; Treherbert 27/10/29; Cathays 24/11/29; Treherbert 22/12/29; Radyr 14/3/31; Treherbert 11/4/31; Barry 1/44; Treherbert 3/44; Cardiff East Dock 17/5/47; Treherbert 14/6/47; Cathays 15/5/48; Treherbert 12/6/48; Abercynon 22/3/52; Cathays 30/1/54; Abercynon 27/2/54; Aberdare 8/9/62; **wd 2/12/63; sold to T W Ward, Briton Ferry 28/2/74; mileage 822,563**

5681 Barry 16/10/26; Coke Ovens 28/10/28; Cae Harris 7/5/32; Radyr 4/6/32; Cathays 1933; Barry 9/41; Cathays 10/41; Merthyr 5/42; Cathays 7/42; Barry 8/44; Cathays 10/44; Merthyr 8/45; Cathays 9/45; Merthyr 13/7/46; Cathays 10/8/46; Merthyr 25/1/47; Cathays 22/3/47; Merthyr 14/6/47; Cathays 12/7/47; Radyr 6/9/47; Cathays 29/11/47; Merthyr 4/12/54; Rhymney 28/11/64; **w/d 7/5/65; sold to R S Hayes, Bridgend 16/6/65; mileage 775,770**

5682 Barry 17/11/26; Coke Ovens 28/10/28; Radyr 11/4/31; Coke Ovens 1933; Abercynon 13/1/34; Barry 11/43; Abercynon 1/44; Cathays 18/5/46; Abercynon 15/6/46; Barry 21/2/48; Abercynon 20/3/48; **w/d 7/5/62; cut up 8/9/62; mileage 772,623**

5683 Cathays 27/10/26; Rhymney 25/12/27; Dowlais Central 13/5/28; Rhymney 10/6/28; Dowlais Central 2/9/28; Rhymney 30/9/28; Cae Harris 24/8/35; Rhymney 14/11/35; Merthyr 8/1/38; Cathays 5/43; Merthyr 6/43; Barry 3/44; Merthyr 5/44; Cathays 9/44; Merthyr 10/44; Cathays 8/45; Merthyr 10/45; Barry 29/12/45; Merthyr 23/3/46; Cathays 22/2/47; Merthyr 22/3/47; Cathays 14/6/47; Merthyr 12/7/47; Barry 2/10/48; Merthyr 27/11/48; Cathays 7/10/50; Radyr 28/12/57; **w/d 10/3/64; cut up 16/5/64; mileage at 28/12/63 881,103**

5684 Neath 28/10/26; Cathays 20/3/27; Abercynon 28/10/28; Cathays 11/1/36; Abercynon 8/2/36; Cathays 7/43; Barry 9/43; Oxley 15/6/46; Tyseley 2/11/46; Oxley 30/11/46; Tyseley 20/3/48; Oxley 15/5/48; Radyr 25/1/58; Treherbert 12/7/58; Oxley 7/9/63; Tyseley 21/3/64; **w/d 17/7/65**

5685 Cardiff Canton 8/1/27; St Philips Marsh 20/1/29; Newport Ebbw Jct 15/2/30; Cardiff Canton 10/5/30 Newport Ebbw Jct 7/6/30; Aberbeeg 24/10/31; Newport Ebbw Jct 13/2/32; Aberdare 7/5/32; Newport Ebbw Jct 4/6/32; Cathays 24/9/32; Aberbeeg 22/10/32; Newport Ebbw Jct 14/11/36; Abercynon 9/1/37; Aberbeeg 5/2/38; Cardiff Canton 2/4/38; Aberbeeg 26/3/55; Cardiff Canton 19/4/58; Barry 3/12/60; Cardiff Canton 9/9/61; Abercynon 11/8/62; **w/d 14/2/64; cut up 18/4/64; mileage 729,653**

5686 Cathays 15/1/27; Barry 20/2/27; Abercynon 28/10/28; Cathays 9/5/31; Aberbeeg 6/6/31; Merthyr 24/7/37; Abercynon 21/8/37; Barry 11/12/37; Merthyr 6/41; Abercynon 7/41; Cathays 4/43; Abercynon 5/43; Treherbert 6/43; Abercynon 10/43; Treherbert 18/5/46; Abercynon 15/6/46; Rhymney 28/11/64**; w/d 8/3/65; sold to Birds, Bynea 8/4/65; mileage at 28/12/63 822,503**

5687 Barry 14/1/27; Cae Harris 20/3/27; Radyr 9/6/29; Treherbert 1933; Ferndale 28/7/34; Treherbert 12/1/35; Ferndale 9/2/35; Cathays 4/5/35; Abercynon 1/5/37; Barry 26/6/37; Merthyr 21/8/37; Cathays 2/41; Abercynon 5/42; Barry 9/42; Cathays 11/42; Merthyr 12/42; Treherbert 11/45; Cathays 29/12/45; Merthyr 19/4/47; Barry 14/6/47; Cathays 12/7/47; Cardiff East Dock 20/4/57; Radyr 28/12/57; Treherbert 12/7/58; Merthyr 29/12/62; **w/d 2/12/63; sold to Birds, Morriston 28/2/64; mileage 766,561**

5688 Cathays 20/12/27; Radyr 27/11/27; Treherbert 30/9/28; Barry 23/12/28; Swansea East Dock 1933; Duffryn Yard 4/5/35; Cathays 2/45; Treherbert 3/45; Abercynon 15/6/46; Treherbert 5/10/46; Barry 17/5/47; Cardiff East Dock 14/6/47; Treherbert 12/7/47; Barry 9/8/47; Treherbert 6/9/47; Abercynon 20/4/63; Rhymney 28/11/64**; w/d 3/6/65; sold to T W Ward, Briton Ferry 28/7/65; mileage at 28/12/63 850,981**

5689 Cathays 15/1/27; Coke Ovens 30/10/27; Barry 23/12/28; Cathays 12/4/30; Barry 10/5/30; Westbury 20/12/30; Swindon 30/4/38; Westbury 4/44; Barry 23/2/63; Radyr 5/9/64; **w/d 21/5/65; sold to Birds, Morriston 24/6/65; mileage at 28/12/63 562,200**

5690 Cathays 20/1/27; Rhymney 25/12/27; Barry 1/9/29; Rhymney 29/9/29; Cathays 17/12/32; Rhymney 1933; Cathays 20/8/38; Merthyr 17/9/38; Chester 1/43; Shrewsbury 6/11/54; Tondu 21/5/59; **w/d 1/8/63; sold to R S Hayes, Bridgend 1/1/64; mileage 642,058**

5691 Cathays 20/1/27; Rhymney 20/3/27; Dowlais Central 10/7/27; Rhymney 7/8/27; Dowlais Central 30/10/27; Rhymney 27/11/27; Treherbert 28/10/28; Cardiff Docks 20/1/29; Treherbert 17/2/29; Merthyr 10/41; Treherbert 11/41; Abercynon 6/43; Treherbert 7/43; Barry 5/44; Treherbert 7/44; Barry 20/4/46; Cardiff East Dock 18/5/46; Treherbert 15/6/46; Cathays 12/7/47; Treherbert 9/8/47; Cathays 29/11/47; Treherbert 27/12/47; Abercynon 23/3/63; Radyr 28/11/64; **w/d 25/6/65; sold to R S Hayes, Bridgend 28/7/65; mileage at 28/12/63 785,992**

5692 Cathays 20/1/27; Radyr 20/2/27; Rhymney 20/3/27; Cathays 4/7/31; Rhymney 24/9/31; Dowlais Central 15/11/34; Rhymney 12/1/35; Cathays 9/41; Merthyr 10/41; Barry 23/3/46; Merthyr 18/5/46; Cathays 7/10/50; Radyr 28/12/57; Treherbert 12/7/58; Radyr 27/12/58; Llanelly 10/9/60; Tondu 11/7/63; Radyr 18/4/64; **w/d 21/7/65; sold to J Cashmore, Newport 6/9/65; mileage at 28/12/63 885,770**

5693 Swindon 20/1/27; Llanelly 20/3/27; Cathays 15/5/27; Cardiff Radyr 7/8/27; Cathays 2/10/27; Radyr 30/10/27; Cathays 27/11/27; Treherbert 25/12/27; Barry 17/3/29; Treherbert 14/4/29; Barry 12/4/30; Cathays 10/8/46; Barry 30/11/46; Treherbert 17/6/50; **w/d 14/1/63; sold to R S Hayes, Bridgend 26/8/63; mileage 753,425**

5622 alongside the rebuilt Barry engine shed, after overhaul and repainting in lined green, in 1958 maybe. Behold the rarely-spotted right-hand lion in the emblem! It was officially discarded in late 1958. The tank weld line made for a difference in texture and flatness and subsequent weathering, often quite spoiling the emblem, whichever way the lion was facing. The oil pipe to the smokebox regulator is running *outside* the boiler casing to the tapered smokebox cover. This should indicate a temporary arrangement but it had been in this state since at least the summer of 1956 so the 'temporary' piping had survived an overhaul and repainting! S.B. Lee, ColourRail.

5627 with a typical train, coal in a motley collection of wagons on a Target working, at Penrhos Junction on 4 October 1957. S. Rickard J&J Collection, D.K. Jones.

5694 Cathays 7/2/27; Cae Harris 20/3/27; Cathays 9/5/31; Cae Harris 6/6/31; Cathays 4/5/35; Cae Harris 1/6/35; Merthyr 21/9/35; Cae Harris 19/10/35; Cathays 15/10/37; Merthyr 4/41; Cathays 10/43; Barry 9/45; Merthyr 10/45; Neath 23/3/46; Merthyr 20/4/46; Barry 13/7/46; Merthyr 10/8/46; Cardiff East Dock 9/8/47; Merthyr 4/10/47; Cathays 15/5/48; Merthyr 12/6/48; Treherbert 21/4/56; Radyr 21/3/64; **w/d 13/11/64; sold to R S Hayes, Bridgend 12/1/65; mileage at 28/12/63 729,276**

5695 Cathays 5/2/27; Cae Harris 20/3/27; Treherbert 22/11/30; Cathays 3/4/37; Treherbert 1/5/37; Barry 1/42; Treherbert 2/42; Barry 8/42; Treherbert 9/42; Cathays 1/45; Treherbert 3/45; **w/d 18/12/62; sold to J Cashmore, Newport 6/63; mileage 799,872**

5696 Cathays 5/1/27; Cae Harris 20/3/27; Rhymney 9/5/31; Cathays 28/7/34; Rhymney 25/8/34; Cathays 16/11/35; Rhymney 14/12/35; Dowlais Central 4/4/36; Rhymney 2/5/36; Cathays 20/8/38; Merthyr 4/41; Cathays 5/42; Merthyr 7/41 Barry 11/41; Barry 8/43; Merthyr 9/43; Barry 1/45; Merthyr 2/45; Cardiff East Dock 23/3/46; Cathays 20/4/46; Merthyr 18/5/46; Barry 2/11/46; Merthyr 28/12/46; Cardiff East Dock 14/6/47; Merthyr 12/7/47; Barry 4/10/47; Merthyr 1/11/47; Rhymney 28/11/64; **w/d 7/5/65; sold to R S Hayes, Bridgend 16/6/65; mileage at 28/12/63 854,297**

5697 Cathays 3/2/27; Cae Harris 20/3/27; Cathays 19/12/31; Radyr 19/11/32; Landore 1933; Duffryn Yard 4/41; Gloucester 17/5/47; Duffryn Yard 20/3/48; Cathays 16/7/49; Didcot 5/9/53; Oxford 8/8/59; St Philips Marsh 26/3/60; Didcot 21/5/60; Radyr 13/8/60; **w/d 25/4/63; sold to J Cashmore, Newport 7/11/63; mileage 649,272**

5698 Cathays 9/2/27; Cae Harris 20/3/27; Barry 1/9/29; Radyr 27/10/29; Treherbert 22/12/29; Merthyr 8/43; Cathays 11/43; Merthyr 12/43; Barry 11/44; Merthyr 12/44; Cathays 14/6/47; Merthyr 9/8/47; Cathays 1/11/47; Merthyr 29/11/47; Cathays 12/6/48; Merthyr 10/7/48; Aberdare 5/9/53; **w/d 21/9/62; cut up at Caerphilly Works 26/1/63; mileage 742,123**

5699 Cathays 5/2/27; Cae Harris 20/3/27; Barry 22/12/29; Abercynon 17/5/47; Barry 14/6/47; Treherbert 15/5/48; Barry 12/6/48; Abercynon 4/11/50; Radyr 28/11/64; **w/d 13/11/64; sold to R S Hayes, Bridgend 12/1/65; mileage at 28/12/63 730,587**

Main sources are the GWR/WR allocation records up to the end of 1963 held at the National Archives, Kew and the RCTS *Railway Observer*. I must thank in particular Maurice Dart who checked the original draft and was able to make a number of corrections. In BR days locos at Merthyr sub-sheds were not listed separately.

A number of 0-6-2Ts shown at Neyland actually worked from Whitland and this has been amended so, based on Maurice's records.

5630 with a Valley lines passenger service at Treforest in August 1957. Norman Preedy.

Seen earlier (page 16) in a closer view, 5633 makes for a pretty portrait, at Treherbert shed on 29 August 1964. The engine lasted into the following year. Ken Fairey, ColourRail

More empties behind an 0-6-2T; 5634 near Bargoed about 1964 in typical Valley country, industry only barely keeping nature at bay. Michael Boakes Collection.

5641 runs into Abercynon from Merthyr with working 'JD' on 8 August 1957. The bunker tank vent pipe runs up in usual fashion. S. Rickard J&J Collection, D.K. Jones.

Lined green on 5642, ex-works at Cardiff Canton on 8 November 1959. Tank top lubricator gone. Norman Preedy.

5658 at Birmingham Snow Hill, probably about September 1958 having newly transferred from Stourbridge. Michael Boakes Collection.

5659 at Pontllanfraith where the line runs east-west from the Sirhowy to the Rhymney valley, about 1964. A.E. Durrant, Michael Boakes Collection.

Toolbox-fitted 5660 at Rhymney shed in the rain on 13 September 1951. Behind is another 5600 while beyond is Rhymney Railway 0-6-2T 79. 5660 has the 'temporary' oil pipe to the smokebox regulator *outside* the boiler casing to the tapered smokebox cover – see 5622 earlier for instance. Also it has the safety valves peeking above the bonnet. H.C. Casserley, courtesy R.M. Casserley.

5662 at Taff Merthyr (Colliery) Halt heading north towards Bedlinog and Merthyr, August 1963. By now only one track is in use. The colliery on the right was sunk between 1922 and 1924 making it one of the last to be sunk in South Wales under private ownership. The halt appears to have opened in 1924. The pit closed in 1992 – presumably the halt had closed much earlier. The hand painted sign on the fencing seen beyond the last carriage of the train reads FREE WALES. The location was also a stop-off point in the Swansea Railway Circle 'Rambling 56' tour of 31 July 1965. The train was hauled by 6643. A.E. Durrant, Michael Boakes Collection.

Merthyr's 5662 taking water at Bargoed on 25 October 1963 the crew, no doubt, having heeded the warning about its non-availability at Rhymney! Rear cab ventilation doors shut, for a change. L.W. Rowe, ColourRail

5664 sits in line at Barry shed in the late 1950s. The place was home to rows of dead locomotives long before the Woodham yard began to accumulate them and in a curious precursor by 1959 more than twenty pannier tanks were in store, nearly all 57XXs. By some quirk of working the diesel shunters at Cardiff East Dock were working from Barry, making for local redundancies in the shunting fleet. A number of panniers were then brought up to scratch for use on the Southern Region. J. Leaf, ColourRail

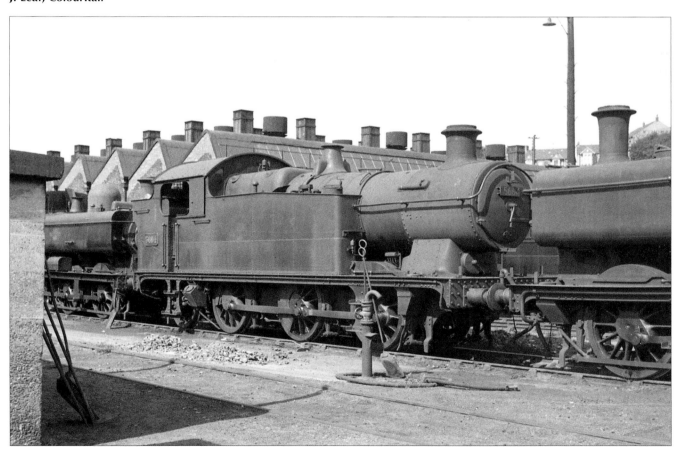

Newly overhauled in lined green, 5667 alongside its Barry home on 16 October 1960. The small upright bottle object in front of the tank is the 'class B' vacuum pump lubricator, as mentioned before. It's a rather better view of it – it supplied oil to the pump cylinder to lubricate the pump piston. Ken Fairey, ColourRail

Dowlais Top, which certainly deserved the name, with 5670 departing on 5 September 1959. The view is looking towards Pontsticill Junction with the southbound train for Newport (next stop Fochriw) about to descend the 1 in 40 towards Bargoed. At this time although it crossed the old LNWR line further south this had been long since lifted. To the left of the line in the foreground, where a more recent brick-built structure stands, until 1933 there was a connection running up to the higher level LNWR line which also had its own 'Dowlais Top' station nearer the town. Spoil heaps from old quarry workings are on the right behind the train. The station closed to goods in March 1961, the whole line to passengers in December 1962 and for goods in May 1964. RailPhotoprint

5671 with a couple of coaches near Bedlinog, probably not far short of a thousand feet up, in August 1963; one track has evidently gone out of use. A.E. Durrant, Michael Boakes Collection.

Dowlais Cae Harris shed yard with lined green 5674 (tall bonnet, tank top lubricator and later pattern vent pipe) resting there on 10 July 1958. H.C. Casserley, courtesy R.M. Casserley.

5673 at Swansea High Street in August 1958. The label in the window of the vehicle immediately in tow reveals it to be the TREHERBERT VAN. A curious chain hangs from the cab next to the sliding shutter. L. Turner, transporttreasury

5678 in black at Radyr shed, 2 August 1953. To the right is Rhymney Railway 0-6-2T 43, withdrawn a couple of years later. Norman Preedy.

5679 negotiates the crossover to the platform at Birmingham Snow Hill, presumably in 1963 when it was briefly a Stourbridge engine before withdrawal. R.G. Fullelove, ColourRail

5680 brings an up goods through Cardiff General station in 1960; rear hand rails not in line with side ones. R.M. Casserley.

In black with first emblem, 5682 sits in the yard at Abercynon shed, 10 July 1958
H.C. Casserley, courtesy R.M. Casserley.

Right. 5687 at Treherbert shed on 19 June 1960, the chimney of the house beyond at first glance appearing to rewrite GW safety valve bonnet history! L.W. Rowe, ColourRail

Below. 5689 at Barry shed on 6 October 1963; the smokebox door lamp iron has been bent entirely out of true and any lamp would shine skywards. Too odd to model!? D. Birt, transporttreasury

Bottom right. A weary-looking 5690, of Chester shed, stands in the wartime ash shelter (later demolished) at Croes Newydd shed on 6 June 1951. The cab front has a relic 'porthole' window, now plated over. A number of the class had started with such portholes, perhaps all of the 5600 series, but they were soon removed/plated over. Unusually for an 0-6-2T, it has acquired a whistle shield – admittedly with a bit of a homemade look about it... Norman Preedy.

Days in the Life of a 5600

Left. 5691 not long out of works, at Treherbert in lined green on 19 April 1958. Ken Fairey, ColourRail

Below left. It is now 1 December 1963 and 5691 has arrived at Swindon awaiting its turn to be traversed into the shops. Since Treherbert in 1958 it has lost the smokebox door lamp iron and instead has a smokebox mounted one. In addition it bears a different, distinctly non-standard number plate. M. Beckett, ColourRail

Below. 5691 now under repair some months later, in Swindon works in April 1964, Warships and Westerns in the background. The loco has now been put in plain black with a new second emblem. It is interesting to see how the main boiler hand rails are split and demounted. A 'proper' number plate has appeared but it looks like the lamp iron will stay on the smokebox top. J.G. Walmsley, transporttreasury

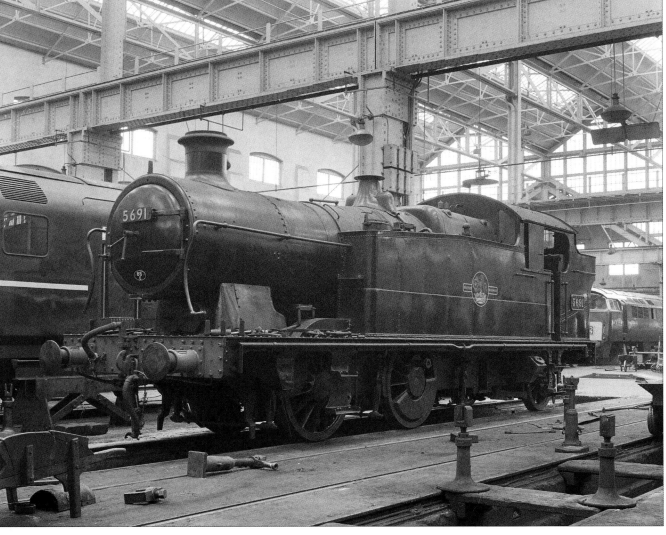

Above. 5696 up in the hills, with assistance from 5671, at Bedlinog in August 1963. A.E. Durrant, Michael Boakes Collection.

Right. 5697 with BRITISH RAILWAYS in Gill sans, helpfully underlined by the horizontal weld, at Cardiff Cathays on 6 May 1951. ATC fitted. H.C. Casserley, courtesy R.M. Casserley.

Top right. 5699 on the coaling line at Aberdare, 16 July 1964; like so many Valley sheds, Aberdare enjoyed a rural, rolling backdrop. L. Turner, transporttreasury

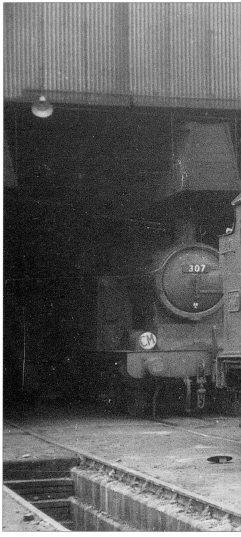

And Finally

Archetypal 0-6-2T Valley coal working. Follow the South Wales 0-6-2Ts through mine and moor in the ongoing *How Green Was My Valley* series (2017-2018) by Nick Deacon in our Irwell Press monthly magazine 'Railway Bylines': *In the cutting below the houses of Taff Terrace, Carnetown (a dormitory suburb to the south of Abercynon) 5682 is held by signals at Carne Parc on 12 January 1960. The engine is heading the Abercynon (88E) J12 target 12.40pm Penrhiwceiber Lower Junction-Radyr Quarry Junction Class J mineral train. To get one's bearings, this unusual view in which the bracket signal emphatically holds centre stage, faces north towards Abercynon on the ex-Taff Vale line and was taken from yet another handy road bridge which in this case carried the road to Abercynon from Pontypridd. To the right, barely a couple of hundred yards away, flows the River Taff. Happily, both the bridge and the railway survive with the latter now carrying a reinstated passenger service as far as Aberdare from Cardiff. 5682 was less fortunate and was withdrawn from Abercynon in May, 1962.* S.Rickard/J.J. Collection.